MEDIUM VOICE

Christmas Solos for All

COMPILED BY JOAN FREY BOYTIM

Christmas Solos for All Ages

ISBN 0-634-03288-7

HAL•LEONARD®
CORPORATION

7777 W. BLUEMOUND RD. P.O. BOX 13819 MILWAUKEE, WI 53213

Visit Hal Leonard Online at
www.halleonard.com

CAROL ARRANGEMENTS

ART SONGS/TRADITIONAL SONGS

POPULAR SONGS

CHRISTMAS SOLOS FOR ALL AGES is a comprehensive book of 45 selections with variable degrees of difficulty. Many of the songs are suitable for beginning teenage singers as well as adults, and some pieces will also satisfy the needs of the advanced singer at Christmas time. The collection is laid out in three categories: art songs/traditional Christmas songs, carol arrangements, and popular Christmas standards.

In order to offer choices for all singers, this volume is published with identical songs in three different ranges, high, medium, and low. The high volume will suit most sopranos and high-voiced tenors. The medium volume has most of the songs not reaching above an F. This will suit the young soprano, the mezzo-soprano, and the medium-voiced tenor and high baritone. The low volume will really address the range needs of altos, baritones, and basses and could provide a useful family song book of solos for the holiday season. The accompaniments range from being very easy to some moderately difficult ones. The majority should prove to be accessible for most accompanists.

This book can be the source of seasonal selections for many types of Christmas programs such as holiday recitals, school concerts, banquets, church services, and seasonal soloist opportunities for service clubs, civic organizations, and other groups seeking holiday entertainment. For ease in constructing programs, in addition to the many religious solos, I have included secular pieces such as "White Christmas," "The Christmas Song," and "Do You Hear What I Hear?" There are solo settings of five of the popular Alfred Burt carols and I have personally arranged new settings of eight lesser known carols such as "The Carol of the Birds," "The Darkness is Falling," "Still, Still, Still," "Mary Had a Baby," and "Rise Up Shepherd and Follow." Included are twelve solos which have been out of print for many years. In addition, the new keys provided for some of the standard solos should be extremely helpful for the studio teacher. Several advanced solos such as the Dello Joio "A Christmas Carol," the Matthews "Voices of the Sky," and the Caldwell "In the Bleak Mid-Winter," join the ever popular "O Holy Night" and "Gesù Bambino."

For the studio teacher, there is enough material in this book to assign it to a student who, through the years, will build a repertoire of Christmas solos to last a lifetime.

Joan Frey Boytim

The Darkness Is Falling

Austrian Carol
arranged by Joan Frey Boytim

1. The dark - ness is fall - ing, the day is nigh gone, I come to a - dore __ thee, the heav - en - ly son. I sing by thy cra - dle a sweet lul - la -

bye, thou art not yet sleep - ing. I hear the soft

cry. Bye - bye, bye - bye, sleep sweet dear - est

child.

2. Now close thy sweet eye - lids, thy cry - ing now

7

As Lately We Watched

19th Century Austrian Carol
arranged by Joan Frey Boytim

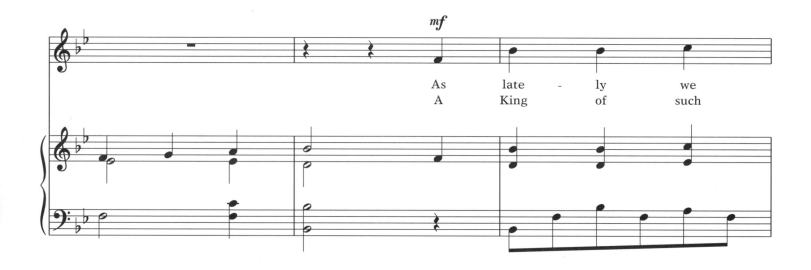

As late - ly we
A King - of such

watched o'er our fields through the night, a
beau - ty was ne'er be - fore seen, and

Carol of the Birds

Traditional Catalonian Carol
arranged by Joan Frey Boytim

Gently, with feeling

1. Up - on this ho - ly
2. The an-sw' - ring Spar - row

night, When God's great star ap - pears, And floods the earth with
cries: "God comes to earth this day A - mid the an - gels

bright - ness. Birds' voi - ces rise in song, And,
fly - ing." Trill - ing in sweet - est tones, The

12

Caroling, Caroling

Words by Wihla Hutson
Music by Alfred Burt

sweet and clear, Sing the sad of heart to cheer.
song we sing, Glad - some tid - ings now we bring.
hap - py morn, "Lo, the King of heav'n is born."

1,2
Ding, dong, ding, dong, Christ - mas bells are ring - ing.

3
Ding, dong, ding, dong,

sub. p

Ding, dong, ding, dong, Christ - mas bells are ring - ing.

mf

Fum, Fum, Fum

Traditional
Catalonian Carol

Joyfully

On this joy-ful Christ-mas day sing Fum, Fum, Fum.

On this joy-ful Christ-mas day sing Fum, Fum, Fum. ___ For a bless-ed Babe was

born up-on this day at break of morn. ___ In a man-ger poor and low-ly lay the

Son of God most ho - ly, Fum, Fum, Fum. Thanks to God for hol - i - days, sing

Fum, Fum, Fum. Thanks to God for hol - i - days, sing Fum, Fum,

Fum. Now we _ all our voic -es raise, and sing a song of grate -ful praise, ___ Cel -e -

brate in song and sto -ry, all the won -ders of his glo -ry, Fum, Fum, Fum.

Go Tell It on the Mountain

African-American Spiritual

Moderate Swing

He Is Born, the Divine Christ Child

18th Century French Carol
arranged by Joan Frey Boytim

He is born the di - vine Christ child,

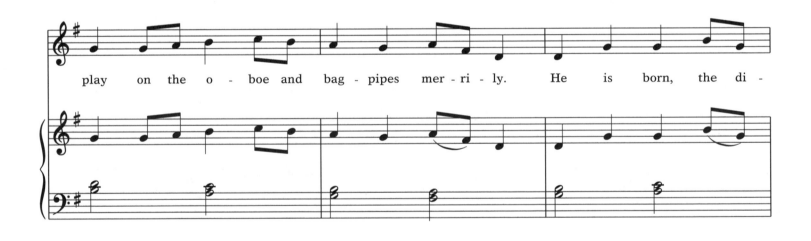

play on the o - boe and bag - pipes mer - ri - ly. He is born, the di -

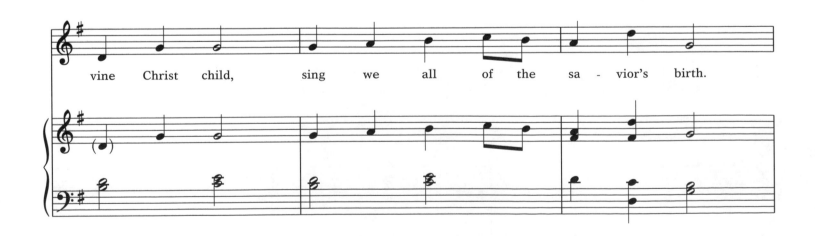

vine Christ child, sing we all of the sa - vior's birth.

Mary Had a Baby

African - American Spiritual
arranged by Joan Frey Boytim

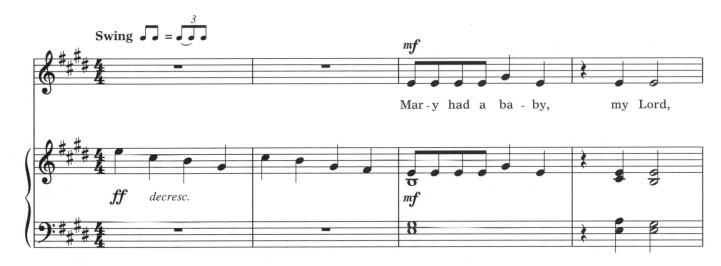

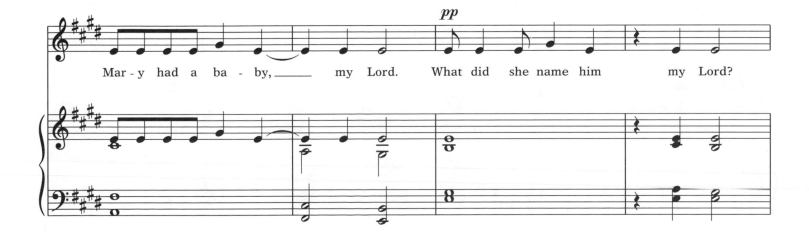

Where was he born _____ my Lord? Where was he born? ___

Where was he born? _____ Where was he born _____ my Lord?

Born in a man - ger _____ my Lord. Born in a man - ger _____ my Lord.

Born in a man - ger, born in a man - ger, born in a man - ger _____ my Lord.

Lo, How a Rose E'er Blooming

Alte Catholische Geistliche Kirchengesäng, 1599
harmonized by Michael Praetorius, 1609

In a traditional style

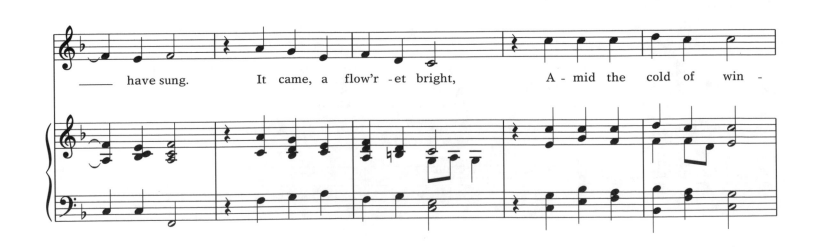

O Come Away, Ye Shepherds

18th century French
arranged by Joan Frey Boytim

O

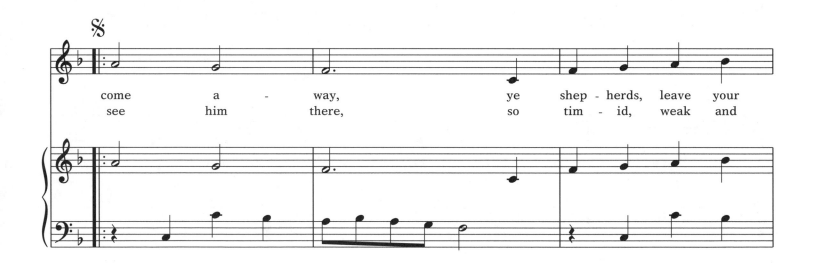

come a - way, ye shep - herds, leave your
see him there, so tim - id, weak and

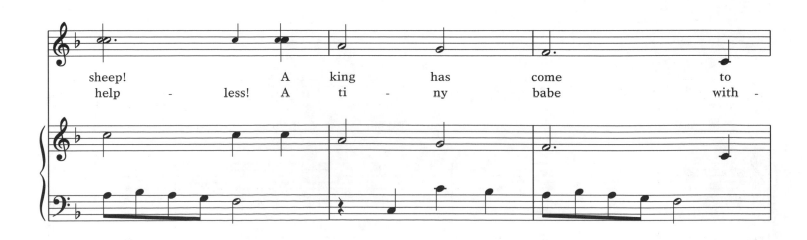

sheep! A king has come to
help - less! A ti - ny babe with -

O Hearken Ye

Lyric by Wihla Hutson
Music by Alfred Burt

1. O
heark - en ye who would be - lieve, The gra - cious ti - dings
heark - en ye who long for peace, Your trou - bled search - ing
heark - en ye who long for love, And turn your hearts to

now re - ceive:
now may cease.
God a - bove.
Glo - ri - a, glo - ri - a In ex - cel - sis

On Christmas Night

Sussex carol arranged by
Ralph Vaughan Williams

33

The Sleep of the Child Jesus

F. A. Geveart

Rise Up, Shepherd and Follow

African-American Spiritual
arranged by Joan Frey Boytim

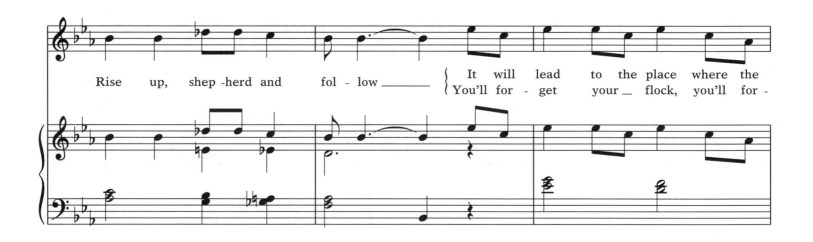

The Snow Lay on the Ground

Traditional Irish-English Carol

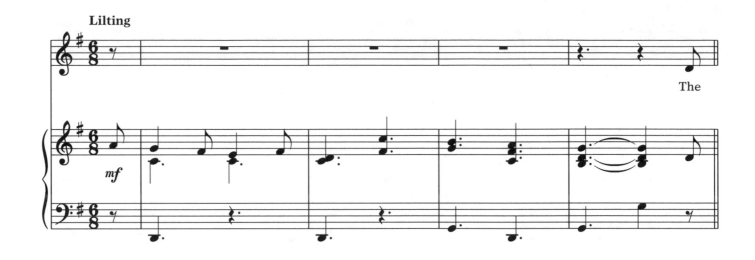

The

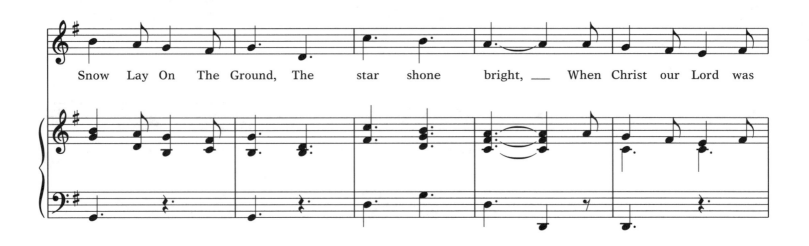

Snow Lay On The Ground, The star shone bright, ___ When Christ our Lord was

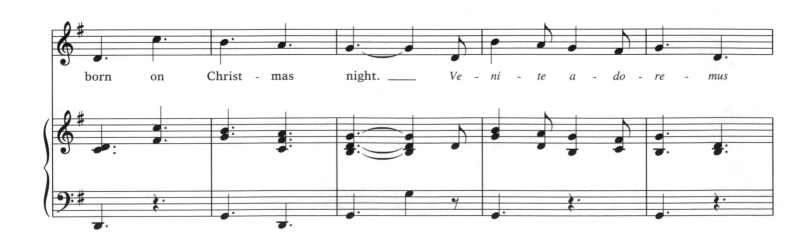

born on Christ - mas night. ___ *Ve - ni - te a - do - re - mus*

The Star Carol

Lyric by Wihla Hutson
Music by Alfred Burt

Sweet - ly a - sleep on a bed of hay.
Shed - ding its light 'round His

lit - tle bed.

Dear Ba - by Je - sus __ ti - ny Thou art,

I'll make a place for __ Thee __ in my heart,

Some Children See Him

Lyric by Wihla Hutson
Music by Alfred Burt

tress-es soft and __ fair.
skin of yel-low __ hue.
filled with ho-ly __ light.

Some chil-dren see Him __ bronzed and brown,
Some chil-dren see Him __ dark as they,
O lay a-side each __ earth-ly thing,

The
Sweet
And

Lord of heav'n to __ earth come down;
Mar-y's Son to __ whom we pray;
with thy heart as __ of-fer-ing,

Some chil-dren see Him bronzed and __ brown,
Some chil-dren see Him dark as __ they,
Come wor-ship now the In-fant __ King,

With
And
'Tis

1,2
dark and heav-y __ hair.   2. Some
ah! they love him __ too!   3. The

3
love that's born to-night!

Still, Still, Still

Melody from Salzburg, c. 1819
arranged by Joan Frey Boytim

Still,_ still,_ still, to _ sleep is _ now his _

will. On Mar - y's _ breast he rests in _ slum - ber, while we _ pray in

end - less _ num - ber, still, _ still _ still to _ sleep is _ now his _ will.

This Is Christmas

(Bright, Bright the Holly Berries)

Lyric by Wihla Hutson
Music by Alfred Burt

Liltingly (♩ = about 63)

1. Bright, bright the hol - ly ber - ries in the wreath up -
2. Gay, gay the chil - dren's voic - es filled with laugh - ter,
3. Sing, sing ye heav'n - ly host __ to tell the bless - ed

on the door, Bright, bright the hap - py fac - es
filled with glee, Gay, gay the tin - sled things __ up -
Sav - iour's birth, Sing, sing in ho - ly joy, __ ye

Bells Over Bethlehem

Traditional
Andalucian Carol

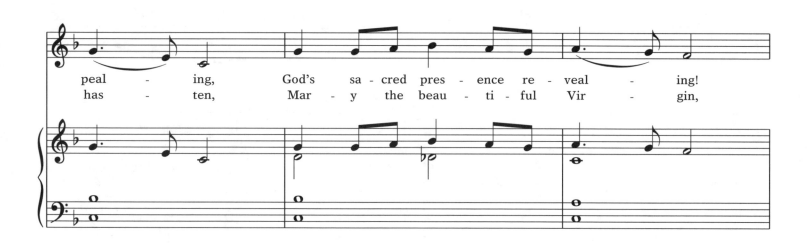

bless - ing!
sleep - ing. } The bells, the bells of Beth - le -

hem Are ring - ing out the ti - dings, "Good - will ___ to all

men!" Leave your sheep _ and come, O shep - herds,

pres - ents bring the Babe so low - ly. ___

8va

L.H.

Bring some cheese and bring some wine ___ For the Moth - er

Mar - y ho - ly. The bells, the bells of Beth - le -

hem Are ring - ing out the ti - dings, "Good - will ___ to all

men!"

8va

8va _ _ _ _ _ _ _ _ _ _ _ _ _ _ _

L.H.

rit.

A Christmas Cradle Song

Words and Music by Bernard Hamblen

Hush thee, my dar - ling, gent - ly sleep, Moth - er her lov - ing watch will keep,

Shad - ows of eve - ning soft - ly creep, Sleep, _ my dar - ling, sleep.

Slow and si - lent, the wear - y day Folds its gar - ments and steals _ a - way,

Dream - land voi - ces are call - ing, Sleep, my dar - ling, sleep,

Ah, _____ Ah, _____

Bells are chim - ing a - cross the snow, Prais - ing His name __ Who,

* - * May be hummed with closed lips

Ah, _____

dim. _pp_

_p_

O - ver the steppe _ and o - ver the town Snow -flakes are weav -ing a

_p_

li - ly - white gown: Je - su, the spot - less, to earth came down:

rall. _p solenne_

Sleep, _ my ba - by, sleep. He Who was born _ that

rall. _p solenne_

The Birthday of a King

W. H. Neidlinger

King.

'Twas a

hum - ble birth - place, but oh! how much God gave to us that

day, From the man - ger bed, what a path has led What a

61

Christmas Candle

Words by Kate Louise Brown
Music by Elinor Remick Warren

dar - ling Christ - Child sweet. _____

He is com - ing in the snow, As he came so long a - go, When the

stars set o'er the hill; When the town is dark and still, He

comes, _____ He comes to do the Fa - ther's will. _____

A Christmas Carol

By Norman Dello Joio

Adagio, con tenerezza

The Christ - child lay __ on Mar - y's lap, His hair was like __ a light. __ O wea - ry, wea - ry were __ the world, but

here, here is all a - right. _____ The Christ-child lay _ on

Mar - y's breast, His hair was like ____ a star, _____ O

stern ____ and cun - ning are ____ the kings, but here the true hearts

are. _____ The Christ-child lay on

68

looked up at Him, and all _____ the stars looked down. _____

O wea - ry, wea - ry were ___ the world, But here the world is a -

right, ___ the world is a - right.

Come to the Stable with Jesus

Words by Daniel Twohig
Music by Geoffrey O'Hara

Jo - seph and Mar - y, the Wise Men and Kings, In

mu - sic our hearts now can share.

Come to the sta - ble and gaze on the scene, The

Christ Child, His beau - ty to share,

Shep-herds are kneel-ing in prayer. Come to the sta-ble with Je-sus to-night, Ah! nev-er a vi-sion more fair! And love Him and wor-ship Him there.

O Holy Night

(Cantique de Noël)

Adolphe Adam

Long lay the world _____ in sin and er - ror
So, led by light of a star sweet - ly
Chains shall he break, for the slave is our

cresc.   *decresc.*

pin - ing, Till he ap - pear'd, and the soul felt its
gleam - ing, Here came the wise men from _____ the O - rient
broth - er, And in his name all op - pres - sion shall

worth.   A thrill of hope the
land.   The King of Kings lay
cease.   Sweet hymns of joy in

cresc.

wea - ry world re - joic - es, For yon - der breaks a
thus in low - ly man - ger, In all our trials is
grate - ful cho - rus raise we, let all with - in us

cresc.

77

CODA

pow'r _____ and glo - ry

ev - er - more _____ pro - claim.

Gesù Bambino

Frederick H. Martens

Pietro A. Yon

an - gels sang, __ the shep - herds sang, The grate - ful earth __ re - joiced, __

__ And at __ His bless - ed birth the stars Their ex - ul - ta - tion

voiced. __ O come let us a -
Opt: Ve - ni - te a - do -

82

Holy Infant's Lullaby

By Norman Dello Joio

Sleep, sleep, _____ O, rest you, ho - ly in - fant, _____ close your

eyes to the star shin - ing bright. _____ Sleep in the arms of your moth - er _____ who

sings to you through the night. A la ru,*) _____ a la me,**) _____ a la

* 'ru' to be pronounced 'roo'
** 'me' to be pronounced 'may'

ru, ___ a la me, a la ru, ___ a la me, ___ a la

ru, a la ru, a la me.

pp

p

con calore *legato*

Sleep, sleep, The

mf

an - gels sing prais - es in heav - en ___ while ___ Ma - ry sings lul - la - by loo. ___

Dream of a day, gen-tle ba-by, _____ when man learns love _ from you. _____ A la

ru, _____ a la me, _____ a la ru, _ a la me, _ a la

ru, _____ a la me, _____ a la ru, a la ru, a la me.

rall. poco

Sleep, _ Ho - ly Child, Ho - ly Child. (Hm)

In the Bleak Midwinter
from *A Christmas Triptych*

Words by Christina Rossetti
Music by Mary E. Caldwell

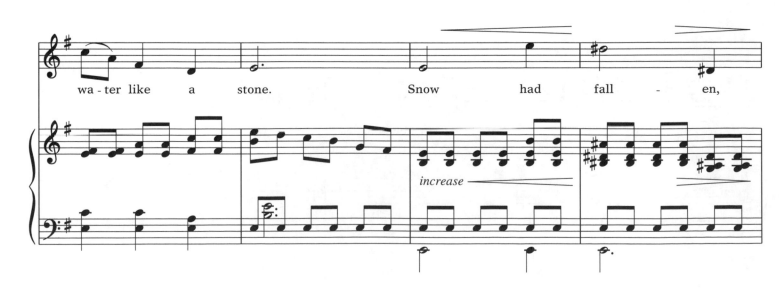

snow on snow, In the bleak -mid -

win - ter, long a - go. Our

God, Heav'n could not hold him Nor _ earth sus - tain;

Heav'n and earth shall _ flee a - way when he comes to reign:

92

Love Came Down at Christmas

Words by Christina Rossetti
Music by Eric H. Thiman

sign. ____ Wor - ship we ___ the

God - head, Love in - car - nate, Love di - vine;

Wor - ship we ____ our Je - sus: But ___ where - with for

sa - cred sign? _____

cresc. poco a poco

O Saviour Sweet

(O Jesulein Süss)

J. Troutbeck and
Helen A. Dickerson

Johann Sebastian Bach

101

The Kings

(Die Könige)

text by the composer
revised by Henry Clough-Leighter

Peter Cornelius

Lento; ben distinto il corale

Three kings have jour-ney'd from the east-ern land, A star hath led them to
Drei Kön' - ge wan - dern aus Mor - gen - land; ein Stern - lein führt sie zum

Jor-dan's strand, And in Ju-de-a, in-quire the three, Where the
Jor - dan - strand. In Ju - da fra - gen und for - schen die Drei, wo

New-born In-fant King may be? With gold and myrrh and in-cense
neu - ge - bo - re - ne Kö - nig sei? Sie wol - len Weih - rauch, Myr - rhen und

Little Noel

(Petit Noël)

Theophile Gautier
English version by
Margaret Aliona Dole

Emile Louis

The night is dark, with snow de-scend-
Le ciel est noir, la terre est blan-

ing,
che;

Bells, gay-ly chime a fes-tal song! _____
Clo-ches, ca-ril-lon-nez gaî-ment! _____

The Christ is born! The Christ is born! _____
Jé-sus est né, Jé-sus est né; _____

a tempo

p

He on the fra-grant hay is sleep - ing, warmed by the breath of
Il trem - ble sur la pa - ille fraî - che, Ce cher pe - tit en -

a tempo

p

friend - ly cow; _____ The ox - en gen - tle watch are
fant Jé - sus, _____ Et pour l'é - chauf - fer dans sa

f

keep - ing A - round the lit - tle Child di -
crè - che L'âne et le bœuf souf - flent des -

f

poco rit.   **Un peu plus lent**

p

vine. _____ The snow up -
sus. _____ La neige au

poco rit.

pp

109

Mary's Slumber Song

Words and Music by Bernard Hamblen

111

slum - ber Thro' the si - lent night, Sleep, lit - tle Lord Je - sus, Till the morn - ing light.

poco rit

pp
a tempo
* Mm _____ Mm _____

a tempo
pp

Mm _____

A lightly open "Ah" may be substituted for humming.

113

The Shepherds
(Die Hirten)

Peter Cornelius
Translation by Henry Clough-Leightner

Peter Cornelius

to mor - tals!"
sie Frie - den!"

Un poco più animato

On - ward the
Ei - len die

shep - herds go,
Hir - ten fort,

cresc. un poco

Haste to the man - ger low,
ei - len zum heil' - gen Ort,

cresc. un poco

Tempo I

Sing - ing praise to the Christ - child, the Sa - viour,
be - ten an in den Wind - lein das Kind - lein,

Sing - ing praise _____ to the
be - ten an _____ in den

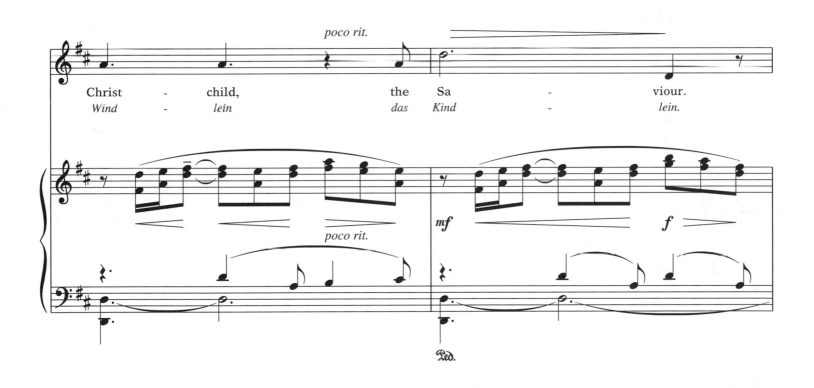

Christ - child, the Sa - viour.
Wind - lein das Kind - lein.

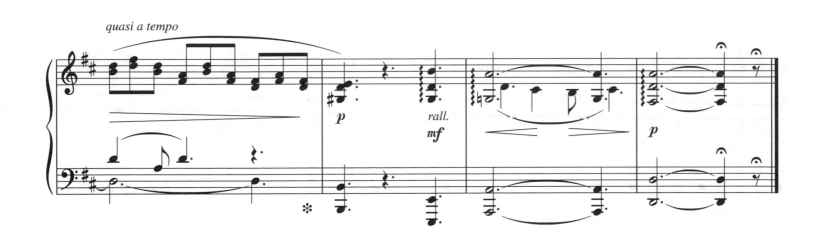

Shepherd's Cradle Song

Words and Music by
C.D. Schubert

121

A Slumber Song of the Madonna

Alfred Noyes

Michael Head

Andante espressivo

Sleep, _____ lit - tle ba - by, I love thee;

Sleep, _____ lit - tle king I am bend - ing a - bove thee! _

How _____ should I know what to sing _____

Here _____ in my arms as I swing thee to sleep? _____

Hush - a - by low, _____ Rock - a - by so, _____

Kings _____ may have won - der - ful jew - els to bring, _____

Mo - ther _____ has _ on - ly a kiss for her king! _____

Why should my sing - ing so make me to weep? _____ On -

- ly I know that I love thee, I love thee,

There's a Song in the Air

J.G. Holland

Oley Speaks

Allegretto con moto

There's _ a song _____ in the air, There's _ a star _____ in the sky, There's _ a moth - er's deep pray'r, And _ a ba - by's low cry; _____ And the star _____ rains its fire _____ While the Beau - ti - ful sing, For the man - ger of

Beau - ti - ful sing, For __ the man - ger of Beth - le - hem __

Maestoso (𝅗𝅥. = 𝅗𝅥)
rit.

cra - dles a King. _____

Allegretto con moto
mf rit.

In __ the

a tempo

light _____ of that star Lie __ the a - ges im-pearled, And __ that

song from a - far Has ___ swept o - ver the world; _____ Ev - 'ry

heart _____ is a - flame _____ While the Beau - ti - ful

sing, In the homes of the na - tions, That

Je - sus is King. _____ We re - joice _____ in the

light _____ And we ech - o the song _____ That comes

down thro' the night _____ From the heav'n - ly

grandioso

throng. Aye, _ we shout _____ to the love - ly _ E -

van - gel they bring, And _ we greet in His

The Virgin at the Manger
(La Vierge à la Crèche)

Alphonse Daudet

A. Périlhou

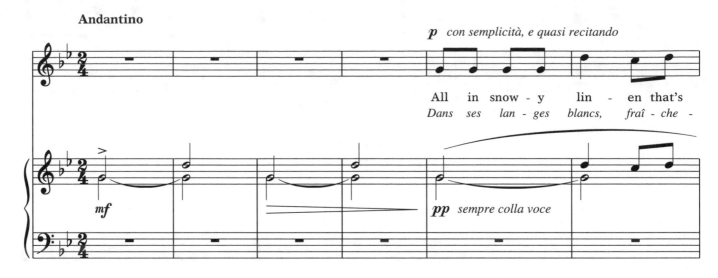

The Virgin's Slumber Song
(Mariä Wiegenlied)

Martin Boelitz

Max Reger

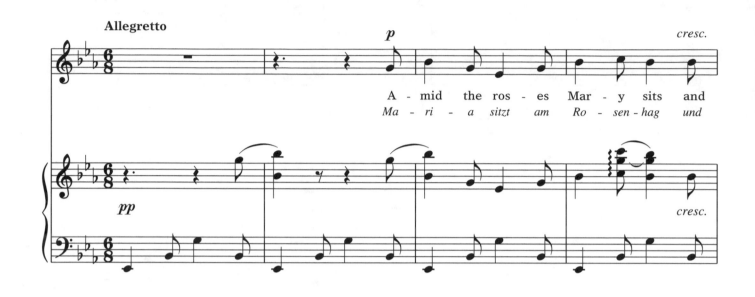

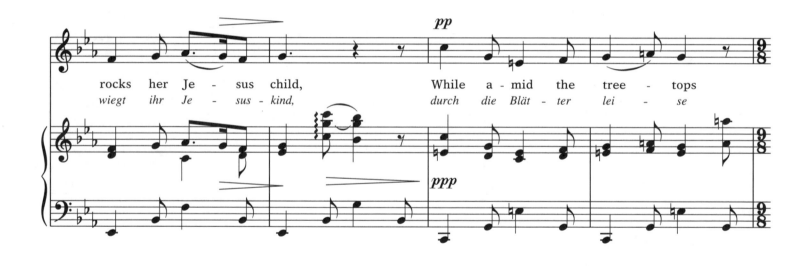

And soft and sweet - ly sings a bird __ up - on the bough;
Zu ih - ren Fü - ssen singt ein bun - tes Vö - ge - lein:

Ah, ba - by, dear __ one,
Schlaf', Kind - lein, sü - sse,

slum - ber now!
schlaf' __ nun ein!

Hap - py is Thy laugh - ter, ho - ly is __ Thy
Hold __ ist dein Lä - cheln, hol - der dei - nes

The Christmas Song

(Chestnuts Roasting on an Open Fire)

Music and Lyric by Mel Torme and Robert Wells

Chest - nuts roast - ing on an o - pen fire,

Jack Frost nip - ping at your nose, yule - tide car - ols be - ing

sung by a choir and folks dressed up like Es - ki - mos. Ev - 'ry - bod - y

knows a tur-key and some mis-tle-toe help to make the sea-son

bright. Ti — ny tots with their eyes all a-glow will

find it hard to sleep to-night. They know that San - ta's on his

way; he's load-ed lots of toys and good-ies on his sleigh, and ev-'ry

Voices of the Sky
from *The Story of Christmas*

H. Alexander Matthews

What Songs Were Sung

By John Jacob Niles

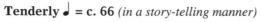

Tenderly ♩ = c. 66 (in a story-telling manner)

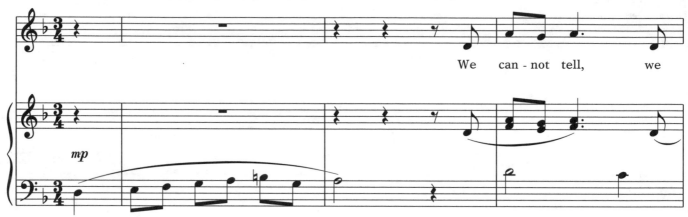

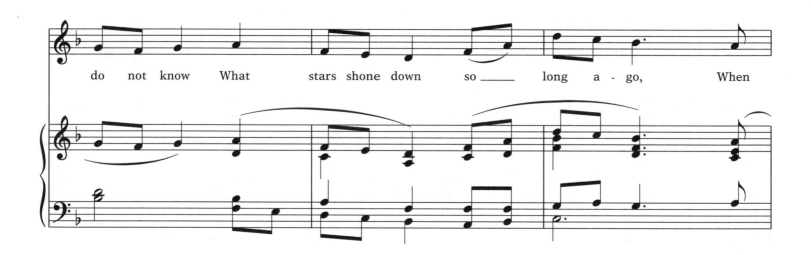

came as one. The Son of God, as scrip - tures said, Was

Vir - gin born in a ti - ny shed, Where sim - ple shep - herds

stood hard by While heav'n - ly sound filled up the sky.

Now let us stand, un -

152

153

why the ho - ly mys - ter - y stands For so man - y years in

so man - y lands. We can - not tell, we

do not know What stars shone down so ___ long a - go, When Mar - y birthed her

own sweet Son And ___ peace and love be - came as one. ___

White Christmas

from the Motion Picture Irving Berlin's HOLIDAY INN

Words and Music by Irving Berlin

The sun is shin - ing, the grass is green, ___ the

or - ange and palm trees sway. There's nev - er been such a

day in Bev - er - ly Hills, L. A.

But it's De - cem - ber the twen - ty - fourth, _____ _____

_____ and I am long - ing to be _____ up

rit. **Tempo I**

north. _____ I'm dream - ing of a

white Christ - mas, just like the

Do You Hear What I Hear

Words and Music by Noel Regney and Gloria Shayne

Danc - ing in the night, with a tail as big as a kite, With a
High a - bove the tree, with a voice as big as the sea, With a
shiv - ers in the cold; Let us bring Him sil - ver and gold, Let us

1,2

tail as big as a kite. Said the
voice as big as the sea. Said the
bring Him sil - ver and gold.

3

Said the king to the peo - ple ev - 'ry - where,

Lis - ten to what I say! _____ Pray for peace, peo - ple ev - 'ry -

where,　　　Lis - ten to what I say! ____ The

Child;　　The Child,　sleep - ing in the night; He will bring us good - ness and

light,　　　*opt.* He will bring us good - ness and

light. ____